Original title:
Quilled Anthems Beyond the Mermaid Dusk

Author: Swan Charm
ISBN HARDBACK: 978-1-80562-037-2
ISBN PAPERBACK: 978-1-80563-558-1

Requiem of Tidal Whispers

In twilight's hush where shadows creep,
The ocean sings of secrets deep.
Waves lap gently on the shore,
Echoes of dreams forevermore.

Beneath the moon's soft, silvery veil,
Whispers of mermaids tell their tale.
Stars blink overhead in the dark,
Guiding lost souls with faint spark.

Each tide unfurls a timeless lore,
Of sailors bold who seek the core.
The depths hold stories steeped in sorrow,
Of treasures bright and grief to borrow.

As shells collect the memories old,
And currents weave their threads of gold,
The requiem plays through the night,
As nature's chorus takes to flight.

A lullaby for the restless sea,
A hymn to set the wandering free.
In harmony with the world so grand,
The whispers of waves knit a band.

Songs of the Celestial Surf

From distant shores the bards resound,
With melodies that stir the ground.
Each note a wave, each chord a tide,
An opus vast where dreams abide.

The seafoam dances in the air,
Singing songs of joy and care.
Footprints trace the songs of old,
As legends weave through sands of gold.

In harmony, the dolphins play,
Conducting symphonies at bay.
The ocean's breath, a gentle sweep,
Cradles the world, lulling to sleep.

Each crest cascades with whispers bright,
Inviting hearts to share the light.
Together in this breezy mirth,
We find our joy in ocean's birth.

Oh, blessings of the starlit surf,
Your watery hymns remind us of earth.
In every splash, a song we share,
A celestial dance beyond compare.

Echoes Beneath the Starlit Tide

Stars reflect on the ocean's skin,
As waves retreat, the night begins.
In the silence, the cosmos sings,
Of ancient tales and wondrous things.

Beneath the tide, lost voices weep,
Whispers of the secrets they keep.
The dance of light, a fleeting grace,
Guiding lost souls to their place.

Shimmering depths with treasures rare,
Hold echoes of love and despair.
Each ripple carries whispered sighs,
Beneath the vast and endless skies.

As the night drapes its velvet shroud,
The ocean's heart sings soft and loud.
In those echoes, dreams intertwine,
With starlit paths that all align.

For every wave that kisses sand,
A promise blooms across the land.
In the depths where silence roams,
We find the echoes lead us home.

Lullabies of the Celestial Deep

In the cradle of the ocean blue,
Lullabies weave the night anew.
Gentle breezes hum a tune,
Beneath the watchful eye of moon.

Hushed are the tides, wrapped in light,
As shadows dance with pure delight.
The sea surrounds with tender care,
Lulling hearts in its embrace rare.

Bubbles float on the surface clear,
Whispers of calm that draw us near.
Magic stirs within the brine,
In the lull of the world divine.

The starlit canopy drapes low,
While dreams drift softly to and fro.
In the deeps where silence dwells,
Lullabies weave enchanting spells.

Close your eyes, let worries fade,
As ocean's lullabies serenade.
In the deep where all is steep,
Find solace in the secrets keep.

Melodies of the Abyssal Web

In shadows deep where silence dwells,
The whispers weave their ancient spells.
With threads of time, in darkness spun,
The dance of fate has just begun.

Silent tides that ebb and flow,
In hidden realms where secrets grow.
Each echo thrills, a subtle tease,
The songs of depths strike quiet pleas.

A phantom glow, a flicker's chase,
In every wave, a fleeting trace.
The heart of night, so soft and bold,
Unravel truths that must be told.

A swirling mass of twilight's sigh,
With every breath, the worlds comply.
Entwined in time, where spirits rest,
The web of dreams holds every quest.

Chants of the Ocean's Resurgence

Awake, arise, the waters call,
In harmony, we rise or fall.
The whispers swell, a mighty throng,
In tides of hope, we all belong.

The sirens sing of ancient lore,
Of ships that sailed and hearts that soared.
With opened seas, we'll find our way,
Through storms of doubt, to brighter days.

Each cresting wave, a promise made,
In salty air, all fears will fade.
We gather strength, each soul a flame,
United voices, we stake our claim.

From moonlit shores to distant lands,
We weave our dreams with steady hands.
In ocean's heart, we'll chart the course,
With courage fierce, an endless force.

Echoes of Dusk's Embrace

As twilight falls with gentle grace,
The world is wrapped in soft embrace.
In muted tones where colors blend,
A day departs, yet love won't end.

Through leafy paths, the shadows play,
With whispers of the ending day.
The crickets sing, a soothing balm,
In dusk's embrace, the heart feels calm.

A canvas painted rich and warm,
Where night descends to soothe the storm.
The stars emerge, to guide our way,
In every glance, a hope will stay.

With every breath, the night unfolds,
As dreams are spun in threads of gold.
So here we stand, 'neath fading light,
Together still, through endless night.

Trills of the Wandering Waters

O rivers wide, your waters roam,
In wildest paths, you find a home.
With every twist and turn you make,
The tales of life, your song awake.

From mountain peaks to valleys low,
Your journey weaves a tale we know.
With every ripple, laughter clear,
A melody that draws us near.

In gentle streams that softly kiss,
The banks that cradle every bliss.
In fleeting moments, time stands still,
As every silence longs to thrill.

So raise your voice, oh waters bright,
In tranquil hush or fierce delight.
The trills of nature, pure and free,
In every heart, we'll always be.

Refrains of the Midnight Current

In the deep of night, where shadows play,
The whispers of waves drift far away.
Stars twinkle down with secrets to unfold,
And stories of old, in silence told.

The moon, a guardian, shines from above,
Guiding the lost with a tender love.
Each ripple a note in the vast embrace,
Nature's own symphony, a soft grace.

Electric whispers in the salty air,
Mysteries linger, if you just dare.
The sea beneath, alive and bright,
Sings lullabies to the velvet night.

Dreams ride the waves, on a gentle crest,
Hopes set adrift, searching for rest.
Ebbing and flowing, a timeless fight,
In the refrains of this midnight light.

Found in the depths, where wishes bloom,
The heart of the ocean beats in the gloom.
Listen closely, to the tide's soft churn,
The night holds lessons for all who yearn.

Ballads of the Wandering Tides

Tides whisper tales as they rise and fall,
Secrets of sailors, lost to the squall.
Each crest a memory, each trough a sigh,
As the wandering winds dance by.

With every surge, a tale unfolds,
Of treasure and trouble, of brave and bold.
Guided by stars in the darkened sky,
The waves carry dreams, both low and high.

Songs weave through drifts of salt and spray,
Ballads of voyage, night turning to day.
Anchors of time in the ocean's breath,
Lost in the rhythm of life and death.

From rocky shores to the heavens wide,
The wandering tides will ever abide.
They carry our hopes and fears in hand,
Mysteries buried in the soft sand.

So listen, dear traveler, to the sea's soft call,
For within its depths, we flourish or fall.
In ballads of waters, find solace and fade,
With the tide as your guide, be unafraid.

Melodic Waves of the Enchanted Bay

In a bay where whispers blend with light,
Melodies twine like the stars at night.
Waves dance in rhythm, the shore holds tight,
As magic unfolds in the soft twilight.

Crystals of water, glistening bright,
Echo the laughter of the birds in flight.
Each pulse of the ocean, a sweet embrace,
Nature's own music in this sacred place.

Shells strum like chords upon the sand,
Carried by breezes, perfectly planned.
Harmonies play in the cool ocean air,
Melodic waves weave secrets rare.

Every whisper a note, every splash a song,
In this enchanted bay where we belong.
Feel the pulse of the world, in the ocean's sway,
Where time melts away with each dawning day.

So come, gather close, as the night descends,
In the embrace of the bay, where the journey bends.
Melodic waves cradle our dreams with care,
In this symphony vast, we float on air.

Whispers of the Seafarer's Heart

Beneath the calm of a starlit dome,
The sea tells stories, luring hearts home.
Whispers of longing ride on the breeze,
Filling the night with a soft unease.

Rugged sails billow, and hopes take flight,
In the shadows where the waves ignite.
Hearts of seafarers bound by the tide,
Chasing the horizons where secrets reside.

With salt on their lips and sand in their veins,
They dance with the tempest, embrace the rains.
Each crash of the waves, a heartbeat strong,
The whispers of love in the sailor's song.

Across the vast blue, where dreams intertwine,
The rhythm of journeys, a fate divine.
In every sigh, a compass found,
Guiding their spirits on the vastness unbound.

Take heed of the whispers, let your heart chart,
For the call of the ocean dwells deep in your heart.
Seafarer's tales weave through the night,
A legacy born from both darkness and light.

Songs of the Forgotten Ocean

Waves whisper tales of dreams once bright,
Secrets shimmer in the moon's soft light.
Beneath the depths, a world remains,
Where time is lost, and hope sustains.

Ghostly ships sail, their sails worn thin,
Echoes of laughter, long since been.
Navigate the shadows, sail the unseen,
Above the dark, where stars convene.

Coral castles in hues of blue,
Guarded by mermaids, wise and true.
They sing of journeys, the paths we've crossed,
In the heart of the sea, no soul is lost.

From ancient tides, the whispers call,
To those who linger, to those who fall.
A bond to the ocean, forever sewn,
In the depths of silence, we find our own.

So drink in the magic, let it seep,
The songs of the ocean, a treasure deep.
For every wave holds a story rare,
In the breeze that lingers, we feel its care.

Ballads of the Darkening Deep

In twilight's gloom, the waters stir,
Chanting secrets that softly blur.
With shadows dancing on the sea,
The darkness sings of what might be.

Beliefs lie buried where sailors tread,
In silence kept, the forgotten dead.
Their voices murmur like a gentle prayer,
In the twilight's grasp, knit tales that dare.

A lighthouse glimmers, a beacon bright,
Against the tempest, against the night.
Yet deep below, where few would roam,
The spirits of the lost call home.

With every wave, a promise made,
In the depths where the memories fade.
The ocean holds its truths so dear,
Whispers of wisdom only few can hear.

So heed the ballads of the deep's embrace,
In the murky waters, find your grace.
For in the darkness, hope is spun,
In the heart of the deep, we are as one.

Echoes from a Distant Shore

From cliffs of stone to sandy bays,
Where sunlight dances in playful ways.
There lies a whisper, soft and clear,
Echoes from places far and near.

Seagulls call in the morning light,
Guiding wanderers, lost from sight.
With each breath of salt, a world unfolds,
A tapestry woven with stories bold.

Castles crumbled beneath the tide,
Memories of legends, where time did bide.
Amidst the shells scattered on the ground,
Those stories linger, quietly profound.

In twilight's glow, the echoes swell,
Carrying tales that the sea will tell.
A harmony sweet, both old and grand,
From the depths of the ocean, hand in hand.

So walk the shore, where echoes play,
Let the whispers guide you on your way.
For every wave that kisses land,
Holds echoes of dreams, by destiny planned.

Verses of the Ethereal Sea Breeze

Through sapphire seas, the breezes sway,
Gentle caresses that drift away.
With every gust, a tale unfolds,
Of hidden realms and treasures untold.

The sailboats glide, their sails unfurl,
Carrying dreams to a distant swirl.
The breeze speaks softly, urging them forth,
To find their place on this vast earth.

A chorus of waves in rhythmic dance,
Inviting hearts to take the chance.
In the embrace of the soothing air,
We find our courage, laid bare.

As starlit skies cloak the sailing night,
The breeze whispers secrets, soft and light.
A lullaby carried on the tide,
Where hopes and wishes quietly reside.

So pause and listen, breathe it in,
The magic of the breeze, let it spin.
For in the whispers of the sea's decree,
We discover the echoes of you and me.

Nocturnal Bliss of the Coral Reefs

In twilight's glow, the corals sway,
As stars peek through the ocean's veil,
A symphony of colors play,
Where moonbeams dance, and dreams set sail.

The fish, they glitter, quick and bright,
In shadows deep, their stories twine,
The soft and gentle touch of night,
A magic spell, so sweet, divine.

Above, the waves, they whisper low,
Secrets dark that times conceal,
Beneath the tides, a world can grow,
A lullaby the sea can feel.

With every breath, the waters hum,
A song of life, both rich and rare,
In this deep home where shadows come,
A peace unfolds beneath the glare.

So let us drift where dreams can roam,
In coral gardens, life will fuse,
For in the depths, we find our home,
A nocturnal bliss we dare to choose.

Hymns to the Mystical Abyss

In the deep blue where silence reigns,
Beneath the waves, the secrets lie,
Whispers of aeons, lost refrains,
A tapestry beneath the sky.

The shadows twist in ancient grace,
As mysteries unfold their wings,
In the abyss, a hidden place,
Where every heart of ocean sings.

For legends vast, the water weeps,
Of oceans wide and realms unseen,
Through darkened depths, the spirit creeps,
To touch the void where dreams convene.

Each current flows with timeless lore,
As echoes of the past resound,
In depths profound, forevermore,
The hymns of mystery abound.

So dive with me, where all is still,
Embrace the depth, the quiet prayer,
For in the abyss, our hearts will fill,
With hymns of life, a bond we share.

Rhythms of the Ocean's Heartbeat

The ocean breathes, a rhythmic song,
With every wave, a pulse reveals,
The dance of tides, both soft and strong,
A heartbeat that the ocean steals.

In whispers soft, the waters sigh,
A lullaby of ebb and flow,
With every rise, a sweet goodbye,
As time within its depths does grow.

Each splash and froth tells tales of yore,
The mariners' dreams, the sirens' call,
In harmony, the secrets pour,
While echoes of the deep enthrall.

So let us listen, hearts attuned,
To every swell, a story spun,
For in these rhythms, life resumed,
The timeless dance of moon and sun.

In ocean's bosom, time can cease,
And every heartbeat sings of peace,
Together, we shall find release,
In rhythms of the sea's embrace.

Odes to the Dreaming Sea

Oh, dreaming sea, with waves so wide,
Your whispers weave through sands of gold,
A canvas vast, where hearts confide,
In stories of the brave and bold.

With tides that pull the moon at night,
And currents that cradle the floss of dreams,
You cradle stars in your soft light,
Reflecting hopes like shimmering beams.

Each ripple sings of worlds untold,
Of sailors lost, of lovers found,
In depths where wonders do unfold,
A magic deep, forever bound.

So let us cast our thoughts and fears,
Upon your waves, so wild and free,
For in your depths, through laughter, tears,
We pen our odes to the dreaming sea.

With every wave that breaks ashore,
In salty kisses, shared delight,
Our spirits soar forevermore,
In harmony, we find our light.

Verses from the Siren's Lure

In the twilight where shadows play,
The siren whispers soft and low,
Her voice a gentle, haunting sway,
Draws sailors to her watery glow.

Beneath the waves, the secret thrums,
A melody of heart's desire,
With every note, temptation hums,
Like a moth that flirts with fire.

Her hair, a cascade of seafoam bright,
Eyes like stars that pierce the night,
She sings of love, of loss, of fate,
But heed the warning, do not wait.

For in her song lies peril's call,
Many have vanished in her tide,
With hopes and dreams, they took the fall,
Lost within the depths, they bide.

So young sailors, stay ashore,
Let not her voice beguile your mind,
For the siren's lure is evermore,
A song of fate that's cruel and blind.

Echoes of the Enchanted Shoreline

Along the beach where magic stirs,
The echoes of the past align,
Soft whispers dance with ocean furs,
In tides that weave a wondrous line.

Each grain of sand a story spun,
Of sailors brave and lovers lost,
Underneath the setting sun,
They paid the sea its fateful cost.

When moonlight kisses waves in flight,
The shoreline breathes a timeless truth,
A canvas splashed in silver light,
Painting dreams of age and youth.

The seagulls cry, a siren's cheer,
While winds caress the water's sheen,
Nature holds what we hold dear,
In every wave, the past is keen.

So wander forth, embrace the shore,
Let every whisper find its way,
For in each tide that comes ashore,
The echoes of our hearts will stay.

Songs of the Glimmering Horizon

As dawn unfolds in hues of gold,
The horizon glimmers, calls the day,
With stories ancient, yet untold,
In morning's light, the past gives way.

Waves breach forth in rhythmic rhyme,
Their song a symphony divine,
Each crest a note, each trough a chime,
A melody of sea and time.

Oceans deep hold wonders vast,
Creatures born of dream and plight,
Through depths of blue, so wild, unsurpassed,
Their songs are woven into night.

When twilight falls and shadows blend,
The horizon whispers soft and clear,
Promises of journeys that transcend,
Awakening all that we hold dear.

So lift your gaze to skies aglow,
Let the ocean's music find its place,
In every wave and gentle flow,
The horizon sings of love's embrace.

Stanzas from the Seafoam Dream

In dreams where sea foam melts away,
A world of wonder waits to bloom,
With every splash, a child at play,
While mermaids weave their tales from gloom.

Through silver mist, the whispers glide,
A symphony of laughter sings,
In every current, joy and pride,
The ocean dances, and the heart swings.

As starlit skies embrace the tide,
The shimmering depths invite the brave,
With secrets hidden deep inside,
Unraveling all that they can save.

So journey forth, let dreams take flight,
In every wave, a story blooms,
For in the dark, there's glimmers bright,
Awash in magic, hope consumes.

And when the dawn brings forth the day,
Remember well the sea's soft hum,
For in its arms, you'll find the way,
To chase the dreams that always come.

Ballads of the Starlit Depths

In depths where shadows softly creep,
The whispers of the night do seep.
Stars twinkle like lost dreams, aglow,
For secrets the ancient waters know.

Where silverfish and shadows play,
The echoes of the past relay.
Beneath the waves, a world exists,
In shimmering blues, that none resist.

Each sigh a story, each wave a song,
In currents deep where we belong.
With every splash, the tales arise,
Like souls that dance beneath the skies.

An ocean's heart, both wild and wise,
Reflects the starlight in its guise.
In every ripple, magic swirls,
As time unfurls and dreams unfurl.

So listen close, ye heart's delight,
To ballads sung in the moon's light.
For in the depths where waters flow,
Eternal mysteries we shall know.

Chants Beneath the Moonlit Tide

By the shore where secrets weave,
The moonlit tides begin to breathe.
With every surge, whispers take flight,
In soft lullabies through the night.

The sandy grains attest to time,
Each wave a note, each song a rhyme.
With tides that rise and gently fall,
The ocean sings its sacred call.

Listen well to the siren's plea,
For shadows dance in harmony.
The night enfolds with gentle grace,
As star-kissed winds begin to lace.

Beneath the silver's tranquil glow,
The chants of water ebb and flow.
In fervent whispers, hearts concede,
To tales of love and souls in need.

So wander forth, ye dreamer bold,
Let ocean's magic unfold.
For in the tide's embrace so wide,
Lie heartfelt chants, the universe tied.

Serenades of the Hidden Shore

Where soft sands kiss the ocean's edge,
A hidden shore, a sacred pledge.
With every swell, the lovebirds croon,
Their serenades beneath the moon.

In twilight's glow, sweet secrets hum,
As twilight waves break, slowly come.
The shells await, their stories gleam,
In every grain, a whispered dream.

The breeze carries echoes of the past,
Of fleeting moments, too swift to last.
With every note, the heartstrings sway,
In harmony with the sea's ballet.

And as the stars begin to gleam,
The ocean's heart plays a solemn theme.
Each cresting wave, a lover's sigh,
In serenades that never die.

So linger long on this hidden shore,
Embrace the tides, forever more.
For love's sweet song shall ever be,
A timeless dance by the endless sea.

Melodies of the Siren's Call

In twilight's breath, where shadows blend,
The sirens sing, their voices lend.
A haunting tune that beckons near,
With melodies sweet enough to fear.

Their laughter tinkles like silver bells,
In the silent swell where magic dwells.
Each note a thread, weaving a trance,
A glorious, mystic, timeless dance.

So sailors heed, their hearts aflame,
For darkness cloaks both joy and shame.
Yet still they drift, enticed and drawn,
To the sirens' hymn, at break of dawn.

With siren's song, the waves do crash,
As dreams collide in a swirling flash.
With every heartbeat, danger calls,
In shimmering depths where twilight falls.

So sail ye forth with courage high,
To chase the echoes beneath the sky.
For in their call, the ocean's thrall,
Awaits the brave who dare to fall.

Trills of the Elysian Tides

In twilight's gentle breath, they sing,
The waves weave tales of a forgotten spring.
Stars above twinkle in sweet embrace,
While secrets of the sea drift on with grace.

Whispers of coral, bright and bold,
Echo through waters, treasures untold.
Dancing shadows in a rhythmic swell,
Calling to sailors, enchanted by spell.

A melody born from depths so profound,
Where dreams and realities intermingle around.
Echoes of laughter, soft as a sigh,
Carry the stories of those who fly.

With each rising tide, a new world unfolds,
As mysteries wrapped in the oceanic folds.
The moonlight glimmers on waves that twine,
Binding the hearts of the land and divine.

So hear the trills, let the magic reveal,
The songs of the tides that forever appeal.
For within these waters, hope finds its way,
In the trills of the Elysian sway.

Echoes of the Dusklit Horizon

As day yields softly to night's sweet embrace,
Whispers of twilight stroke time's gentle face.
Horizon bleeds colors from dusk to the deep,
While shadows of stories awaken from sleep.

Beneath the vast canvas, dreams softly dance,
Entwined in the silence, the stars take their chance.
Each twinkle a secret, a memory sighed,
Floating on whispers of the night tide.

In the rich hues of purple, gold, and blue,
Echoes resound, as the world turns anew.
Songs of the ancients, soft as the breeze,
Guide hearts like lanterns through the unfurling trees.

Magic unfolds as shadows take flight,
In the embrace of the dusklit night.
Each heartbeat a rhythm, a life yet unfurled,
As echoes entwine with the mysteries swirled.

So linger a moment in the twilight glow,
Where echoes of dreams in the hearts overflow.
For each dusklit horizon holds tales to explore,
As night wraps the world, forevermore.

Sagas of the Uncharted Waters

In the heart of the ocean, where legends reside,
Sagas are woven in the ebbing tide.
With sails unfurled towards the vast unknown,
Brave souls seek treasures where wild winds have blown.

Wide skies above, with a promise of flight,
Adventures awaken under the soft starlight.
Time tells the stories of those gone before,
Whispers of courage on distant shores.

The waves cry out with the voices of kin,
Of tails long forgotten where dreams might begin.
To sail forth with courage, to dare to believe,
Is the greatest adventure that we can conceive.

Each keening gull echoes the call to explore,
Through tempest and calm, through the wide-open door.
For amidst the chaos, the calm shall arise,
And the heart of the sailor will reach for the skies.

So heed the soft murmurs of the uncharted seas,
Each wave tells a tale carried forth by the breeze.
Within every journey, a spark ignites bold,
In the sagas of waters, the brave shall be told.

Harmonies of the Coral Moon

By the light of the coral moon's gentle glow,
The sea sings of whispers we long to know.
With each ebb and flow, the night starts to weave,
Enchanting the dreamers who dare to believe.

Tides murmur softly, a tender embrace,
Wrapped in the warmth of the ocean's vast space.
Stars wink like jewels as the night unfolds,
Tales from the depths in shimmering molds.

Under the moonlight, colors come alive,
Inspired by stories that dwell and survive.
The coral blooms dance as the rhythm grows,
Filling the night with the magic it knows.

In the symphony played with the moon's silver beams,
Every heartbeat echoes the tune of our dreams.
Embraced by the waters, we wander so free,
Harmonies ripple, a part of the sea.

So listen closely, let the lullabies guide,
To the heart of the oceans where the mysteries bide.
In the glow of the coral moon, we shall find,
The legacies left woven deep in mankind.

Tides of the Shimmering Horizon

Whispers of the ocean's breath,
Call to the hearts that yearn for rest.
Beneath the gaze of the fading sun,
Waves reveal what was once begun.

Colors dance in twilight's fold,
Stories of the brave and bold.
Secrets hidden in the foam,
Stealing dreams far from home.

Shadows play on shimmering waves,
Echoes of forgotten graves.
Every tide a tale unfolds,
In the ocean's arms it holds.

Stars awaken in the night,
Guiding sailors toward the light.
Paths unseen in the shifting sand,
Mapped by the touch of a gentle hand.

Horizon glows with a mystic charm,
Calling to the lost, a solemn balm.
In the stillness, magic thrives,
As the ocean breathes and strives.

Odes to the Abandoned Shores

Lonely sands where sea meets land,
Whispers of time, a soft demand.
Shells and stones, forgotten dreams,
Under the sun, they glimmer and gleam.

Footsteps fade by the water's edge,
Secrets kept in nature's pledge.
Dance of tides, a waltz so sweet,
Time stands still, where memories meet.

Gulls cry out in the salt-kissed air,
Echoes linger of those who dare.
To chart their course on rugged shores,
In search of freedom, they became explorers.

The lighthouses stand, weary and tall,
Guardians of secrets, they witness all.
With every beacon's steady light,
Counting the moments, into the night.

Rustling leaves of the ancient trees,
Whisper tales carried by the breeze.
In solitude, beauty finds a way,
Odes to shores where spirits play.

Sonorous Calls of the Enchanted Reef

Beneath the waves, in colors bright,
Corals whisper, a painter's delight.
Mysteries swirl in aqua depths,
Calling adventure with whispered breaths.

Fish dart by in a playful race,
Nature's art in its finest grace.
Songs of whales in the briny deep,
Echo stories that drift to sleep.

Ocean's harmony, a gentle hum,
Where every creature is welcome to come.
Hearts entwined in the deep's embrace,
Finding solace in this hidden place.

Flickering light through the ocean's veil,
Guiding sailors with an ancient tale.
Guardians of the reef watch near,
In their presence, we find little fear.

With each swell, the water sings,
A melody crafted by nature's strings.
In the depths, enchantment thrives,
In the heart of the reef, life survives.

Epics of the Twilight Sea

In the twilight, shadows play,
Where the night meets the fading day.
Waves lap gently against the keel,
In every swell, stories reveal.

Fables woven in the ocean's foam,
Characters lost, around the globe they roam.
From distant lands to shores unknown,
Each tale crafted, each seed sown.

A ship of dreams sails into the night,
Led by stars, glowing bright.
With the moon as its loyal guide,
Braving the seas, riding the tide.

Calm and storm, the dance of time,
Every voyage, a story in rhyme.
Legends born on the bosom of waves,
Treasures found in the hearts of braves.

As the waves keep their sacred lore,
History echoes from shore to shore.
In the twilight, dreams take flight,
The sea's embrace, a wondrous sight.

Rhythms of the Ocean's Heart

Beneath the waves, a world does sing,
A pulse of tides, where dreams take wing.
With whispers soft, the currents flow,
In darkened depths, a mystic glow.

The moonlight dances on silver crest,
A lullaby that grants us rest.
The ocean's heart beats strong and warm,
A timeless force, a soothing charm.

In coral caves, with colors bright,
Creatures dance in the gentle night.
Their stories spun in foam and spray,
Carry magic along the way.

Each ship that sails, each sailor's tale,
Is woven deep with the ocean's veil.
A tapestry of fate and fate's unfold,
In every hue, a dream retold.

So let us listen, let us feel,
The ancient songs that rise and reel.
In rhythms vast, our spirits soar,
Bound forever to ocean's lore.

Fables from the Seafoam Glade

In the glade where sea meets shore,
Fables whisper evermore.
With shells and sand, the tales arise,
Beneath a sea of endless skies.

Mermaids weave their hearts in song,
With golden voices, pure and strong.
The seafoam sprinkles, laughter bright,
In gleaming waves, a pure delight.

A treasure chest of tales untold,
Of stolen dreams and hearts of gold.
The seabirds dance on winds that weave,
In currents swift, they shape and grieve.

In twilight's hush, the stars awake,
As waves recede, new paths they make.
With every tide, a story spun,
In seafoam glades, where dreams are won.

Join the dance, and heed the call,
For in the tides, we rise and fall.
With every ebb and flow we see,
The fables born from the deep sea.

Melodies from the Seagrass Grove

In seagrass groves where shadows play,
Melodies twirl in a mysterious way.
A serenade of nature's own,
Where ocean secrets softly moan.

With gentle strokes of evening light,
The waves compose a song of night.
A symphony of salt and breeze,
Dancing freely among the trees.

The water's whisper, the breeze's sigh,
Echo tales that float and fly.
In every rustle, a note is caught,
Releasing dreams that time forgot.

Through seagrass tall, a path unfolds,
Where laughter lives and joy beholds.
In every sway, a heart's delight,
In melodies of the fading light.

Listen close, let magic weave,
In seagrass grove, believe, believe.
For every note that nature brings,
Is a reminder of life's sweet things.

Verses of the Deep Ocean's Mystique

In depths where shadows seldom grace,
Lies a world filled with hidden trace.
Verses penned in water's lore,
A vast domain forevermore.

Creatures dance in a silent ball,
Their stories echo through the call.
In emerald depths, mysteries bloom,
With each heartbeat, dispelling gloom.

Serpents glide through crystal blue,
Crafting tales that feel so true.
With every ripple, secrets twine,
In languages of sea and brine.

A shipwreck whispers of lost dreams,
In woven nets of glimmering beams.
With ghostly forms that softly play,
In ocean's arms, they drift away.

Across the tides, the legends swell,
Of brave souls caught in love's sweet spell.
Verses rise from the ocean's crest,
In mysteries deep, we find our rest.

Serenade of the Windswept Shores

Upon the sands where shadows play,
Whispers of bygone tales drift near,
The sea's embrace in twilight's glow,
A melody of dreams we hear.

Seagulls dance in the golden light,
As waves rush forth with frothy grace,
Their laughter mingles with the breeze,
Echoing secrets of this place.

The salt-kissed air, a lover's sigh,
In every grain, the time stands still,
Footprints lead to places unknown,
As the heart bends to its will.

Night falls soft, a velvet shroud,
Stars awaken in the vast expanse,
The moon shall guide our wandering paths,
In this enchantment, we entranced.

Here on shores where fantasies weave,
Every tide will speak of lore,
Hand in hand, we'll chase the night,
Until the dawn brings us to shore.

Chronicles of the Moonlit Wave

In the hush of night, where dreams reside,
The moon casts silver on the tide,
Gentle waves with whispers low,
Carry tales from long ago.

A ship adrift where shadows dwell,
With starlit sails that dance and swell,
The ocean's heart beats deep and wild,
In its embrace, adventure smiled.

The night is dressed in shimmering light,
With every crest, a new delight,
From coral caves to shores unseen,
The beauty speaks where few have been.

Yet storms may brew in sapphire skies,
A warning sung in whispered sighs,
But brave the souls who heed the call,
For within the waves, they rise and fall.

Through every tale the sea has spun,
Each journey leads to battles won,
And in the light of dawn's embrace,
We find our dreams, a sacred place.

Ballad of the Coral Dreamers

Beneath the waves where colors blend,
In coral castles, dreams ascend,
The merfolk sing their timeless song,
In ocean's cradle, they belong.

With fins that shimmer, dart and glide,
They weave through currents, swift and wide,
Each note a wish on ebbing tide,
A dance of life, forever tied.

In twilight hush, when stillness reigns,
The melodies stir ancient pains,
For every dream that drifts away,
Leaves echoes in the sea's ballet.

Yet rise they do, through storm and night,
Unbroken spirits, fierce in fight,
Bound by the magic of the sea,
In coral depths, they are set free.

So listen close to the ocean's sigh,
A call to hearts that yearn and cry,
For every dreamer in the tide,
Will find their path, with hope as guide.

Hymn of the Abyssal Twilight

In the deep where shadows weave,
A world concealed, the bold believe,
The twilight whispers tales of yore,
Of creatures vast, forevermore.

With bioluminescent glow,
Mysteries dance, and currents flow,
A symphony of life and fear,
In depths where silence claims the year.

Here giants roam, both fierce and grand,
While schools of fish in colors stand,
Cascading light through darkest places,
Painting dreams on liquid faces.

Yet tread with care on ocean's floor,
For beauty cloaked in legend's lore,
In twilight's grasp, each moment's brief,
A hymn that reveres their belief.

So heed the call of the abyssal night,
For in those depths, the heart takes flight,
Among the tides where echoes reign,
In the ocean's song, forever remain.

Harmonies of the Twilight Aqueduct

Where whispers weave through bricks and stone,
The twilight sings a haunting tone.
Beneath the arching skies so wide,
The secrets of the night confide.

With every ripple, shadows play,
In the cascading hues of gray.
The stars alight in gentle grace,
Each glimmer holds a tender space.

Old echoes linger, calm and deep,
In twilight's arms, the memories sleep.
From ancient springs, the waters flow,
Carrying tales of long ago.

The moon reflects a silver stream,
Where dreams are spun and dancers dream.
A symphony of night begins,
As nature's magic hums and spins.

Awake, the world in shadows brewed,
Embrace the night, the heart renewed.
In harmony, let spirits soar,
Through every note, forevermore.

Laments of the Forgotten Nautilus

In ocean depths where silence sighs,
The nautilus beneath darkness lies.
Once proud, adorned with shells aglow,
Now whispers fade, and tides do flow.

Forgotten melodies of yore,
Ebb with time upon the shore.
The ocean's breath, a gentle wail,
For tales untold, now lost to frail.

Beneath the waves, the stories dwell,
Of seafarers and sea's sweet swell.
In briny depths, their echoes crave,
To rise again, the lost and brave.

Yet time, it dances, swift and sly,
And shadows claim what once could fly.
A nautilus, adrift in dreams,
In twilight's grip, its heart still beams.

So weep, oh waves, for what's forgot,
For treasures kept in deepened lot.
In every sigh, a longing trace,
The nautilus, in soft embrace.

Trills of the Moonlit Harbor

Upon the docks, where lanterns glow,
The night is filled with secrets low.
With trills of laughter, echoes ring,
As sailors spin their tales of spring.

The harbor hums with spectral grace,
While moonlight paints each weathered face.
Against the tide, dreams take their flight,
Beneath the cloak of tranquil night.

With rippling waves, the stories blend,
To distant shores that evening sends.
Each heart, a tune in rhythm's hold,
In harmony, their fates unfold.

The gulls cry out, a soaring sound,
As friendships bloom on hallowed ground.
Together, drawn by fate's sweet string,
In moonlit harbor, voices sing.

So let the night embrace your soul,
With every trill, be made whole.
In twilight's grasp, find solace near,
As magic whispers, ever clear.

Sagas of the Dancing Waves

Upon the sea, where colors clash,
The waves, they rise in a fervent flash.
Each crest a story, bold and bright,
In sagas spun from day to night.

The ocean, vast, a timeless sage,
Holding secrets of every age.
With every crash, the memories roar,
The ancients call from distant shore.

As dancing jewels, the waters gleam,
Within their depths, the visions teem.
A rhythm flows, both wild and free,
In every swirl, a legacy.

Each drop a promise, whispered low,
To those who heed the waves' soft flow.
With courage, rise and stand your ground,
In unity, our fate is found.

So sail beyond, where dreams ignite,
And glide with winds into the night.
For in the heart of stormy graves,
Exist entwined the dancing waves.

Sonnet of the Dusk-Kissed Shores

Upon the sands where shadows play,
The twilight whispers secrets near.
Soft hues of gold, in skies of gray,
A gentle breeze, the night draws near.

The ocean sings a lullaby,
Its ripples dance with starry glee.
As seagulls glide, they soar and fly,
In harmony, they're wild and free.

Each footstep left, a tale untold,
Of lovers lost, of dreams once bright.
The moon, a pendant made of gold,
Casts silver paths of shimmering light.

With every wave that greets the shore,
A promise made, a wish set free.
As dusk unfolds, we yearn for more,
A fleeting glimpse of destiny.

So linger long, dear heart, and trace,
The moments shared, a sweet embrace.
In twilight's glow, there's magic's trace,
A sonnet born in time and space.

Odyssey of the Ethereal Waves

Let sail the dreams upon the tide,
Where seafarers and starlit skies
Do weave their tales, the ocean wide,
In depths where silent mystery lies.

Each wave a story, raw and bold,
Of sirens' call, of shipwrecked lore.
From ancient tales to futures told,
An odyssey forevermore.

Beneath the salt and whirlwind's breath,
The echoes of the past resound.
In depths that dance with life and death,
A magic waits, yet to be found.

And as the night bestows its grace,
The moonlight's path a guide anew.
Far from the shores we find our place,
On waves that sing their song so true.

So journey on, with heart in tow,
To lands unseen and skies unseen.
For every wave will gently show,
The beauty held in spaces between.

Chants of the Luminous Depths

In depths where sunlight dares not creep,
The creatures dance in twilight's veil.
They sing of secrets, old and deep,
And weave their notes like silken trail.

A harmony of life beneath,
With glimmers bright and shadows wide.
Each whisper carries tales of breath,
Where currents flow and dreams abide.

With every pulse, the ocean sways,
As coral gardens sway with glee.
The chants of life, in timeless plays,
Create a symphony, wild and free.

Those lantern fish, with gleaming eyes,
Illuminate the darkened sea.
They bear the weight of ancient ties,
In luminous depths, our hearts agree.

So join the dance, beneath the waves,
Where water holds its rhythmic beat.
In eternal night, life always saves,
A melody, both pure and sweet.

Reveries of the Celestial Lagoon

In lagoons where starlight falls,
The whispers of the night abound.
Beneath the sky, where silence calls,
A magic stirred, a dream is found.

The waters shimmer, soft and bright,
With visions painted by the moon.
Reflecting dreams in silver light,
Each ripple hums a gentle tune.

With every breath, the night grows deep,
Where fireflies alight with grace.
In tranquil hush, the world can sleep,
As time reveals its warm embrace.

So drift upon this sacred sea,
With hearts that dance in cosmic flow.
Embrace the night, be wild and free,
In reveries where love can grow.

In timeless beauty, we shall stay,
Together bound by starlit dreams.
In every touch, in every sway,
Our souls entwined, or so it seems.

Lament of the Starfish Seers

Beneath the waves, their secrets lie,
The starfish sigh, beneath the sky.
With arms outstretched, they seek the light,
In silent depths, they mourn the night.

Each grain of sand tells tales of old,
Of sunsets bright and dreams untold.
They watch the tides with heavy hearts,
As currents pull their world apart.

When storms do rage and tempests call,
The starfish rise, yet fear the fall.
In whispered songs of ocean blue,
They long for shores they've never knew.

Oh, gentle tides, please bring them peace,
Let moonlit beams their sorrow cease.
In starlit nights, they find their way,
And yearn for dawn to light the day.

Eternal watchers of the sea,
Their hearts entwined with memory.
For in the depths, their spirits soar,
As guardian souls forever more.

Whispers from the Coral Abyss

In coral halls, a story flows,
Of vibrant hues and deep-set woes.
The whispers rise like gentle tides,
From ancient reefs where time abides.

They speak of love and battles lost,
Of creatures found, and lives embossed.
With every crack and crevice worn,
The tales of ages long since torn.

Their echoes dance on currents swift,
In shimmering light, they find their gift.
A glimmering truth in playful sway,
In hidden depths, where shadows play.

So listen close, as Neptune weaves,
A tapestry through woven leaves.
In every bubble, laughter sings,
The secrets of the ocean's springs.

The coral whispers, soft and low,
Of mysteries where only few go.
In the gentle sway of tides' embrace,
They tell of life in ocean's grace.

Harmonies of the Dusk's Embrace

As twilight falls, the sea does dream,
In harmony, a silver gleam.
The waves caress the sandy shore,
While stars above begin to soar.

A melody of dusk unfolds,
In whispers soft, a tale retold.
The ocean hums a soothing sound,
Where every soul may lose and found.

The colors blend in twilight's hue,
Each stroke a whisper, deep and true.
The sea-birds cry, a fleeting tune,
Beneath the watchful, crescent moon.

Together, tides and winds unite,
In dances full of pure delight.
The world in quiet slumber lies,
Beneath the velvet starlit skies.

With each soft wave, a prayer takes flight,
For dreams to drift into the night.
In dusk's embrace, all hearts align,
As nature sings, a sweet design.

Reflections in a Marine Mirror

Glimmers form on quiet seas,
As thoughts drift by like summer breeze.
Reflections dance in sapphire light,
A tapestry of day and night.

The ocean's face, a crystal sphere,
Holds ancient echoes, soft and clear.
In every ripple, stories flow,
Of mariners and ships that glow.

With every crest, a moment caught,
In natures breath, the world is wrought.
The surface shines with dreams unturned,
As tales of love and loss are burned.

A mirror holds the heart's desires,
While moonlight stirs the sleeping pyres.
In tranquil pools of azure deep,
The secrets of the sea do keep.

So gaze into the ocean's eye,
Where wonders wait and spirits fly.
For in the depths, reflections gleam,
Awakening the soul's wild dream.

Hymns to the Tantalizing Depths

In shadows deep where secrets lie,
The echoes of the ocean sigh,
A whisper soft, a glimmer bright,
Calling forth the endless night.

Where sirens sing and shadows dance,
In every wave, a fleeting chance,
For those who dare the depths to seek,
Unlock the truths the waters speak.

The coral reefs, a vibrant maze,
In hues that set the heart ablaze,
A tapestry of life unfolds,
As stories of the sea retold.

With every tide, a promise new,
The depths conceal a world askew,
For in the dark, the stars will gleam,
Inviting all to dive and dream.

So heed the call, brave hearts unite,
Embrace the depths, embrace the night,
For in the sea's enchanting sway,
Lies magic waiting, come what may.

Ballads of the Dreamweaver's Coast

On windswept shores where dreams take flight,
The ocean beckons with its light,
A gentle kiss of salt and foam,
Invites the weary soul back home.

Each grain of sand, a story told,
Of adventurers both brave and bold,
The waves whisper secrets soft and low,
As moonlight guides the tides that flow.

Between the dusk and dawn's embrace,
The dreamweaver spins a timeless lace,
Of fantasy and hope combined,
In every wave, a dream defined.

With painted skies and boundless sea,
The coastal breeze sings wild and free,
For those who wander, hearts afire,
Will find their bliss, their one desire.

So walk the sand with open mind,
Let treasures of the sea unwind,
For at the edge where dreams collide,
The heart's true compass will decide.

Limericks of the Midnight Reef

Beneath the waves where shadows play,
The midnight reef dreams night away,
With fish that twirl,
In watery swirl,
It dances till the break of day.

A crab in red, a sight so bold,
Keeps secrets of the deep untold,
With claws like knives,
In ocean lives,
It scuttles 'neath the sunlit gold.

The octopus, sly and astute,
Wears colors vivid, absolute,
With twists and turns,
As fortune churns,
It paints the reef in bright pursuit.

A dolphin leaps, a silver flash,
Through waters where the currents thrash,
With laughter sweet,
It finds each beat,
Of ocean's song, a joyful splash.

So heed the call of midnight's play,
Join in the reef's enchanting sway,
For life below,
In vibrant flow,
Will leave your heart forever gay.

Rhythms of the Glittering Shore

Where golden sands meet azure skies,
The rhythms pulse, the spirit flies,
In every wave, a heartbeat clear,
The shore's sweet melody draws near.

With crashing surf and whispering breeze,
The tranquil sound brings hearts at ease,
As children laugh and lovers sigh,
The shore invites you, come and try.

In twilight's glow, the stars awake,
With gentle light, the night they make,
A symphony of peace bestows,
As moonlight dances on the throes.

The tide retreats, a lover's dance,
A fleeting moment, not by chance,
For every grain of sand we tread,
Holds stories of the past once said.

So wander forth where dreams can soar,
To find the magic on the shore,
For in each wave and breeze you find,
The rhythm of your heart aligned.

Songs of the Luminescent Lagoon

Beneath the stars, the waters gleam,
Whispers of magic in a moonlit dream.
Creatures dance in the silver tide,
Their luminescent glow, a secret guide.

Rippling echoes of laughter and song,
In this tranquil realm, where we all belong.
With every surge, a melody plays,
In the heart of the night, where the spirit sways.

Shadows of trees on the sandy shore,
Guard ancient tales from yonder before.
Mysteries ripple through bubble and foam,
Calling lost souls to find their way home.

Beneath the surface, hearts intertwine,
In currents vivid, our fates align.
Light and shadow in harmony blend,
In the luminescent lagoon, no journey ends.

So let us sail on this gentle tide,
Where the magic of waters will not divide.
Each wave a promise, each splash a vow,
In the glow of the lagoon, we live for now.

Harmonies of the Shimmering Depths

Down below where the sunlight bends,
The water shimmers, the magic tends.
Coral castles, vibrant and bright,
Sing to the stars through the hush of night.

A symphony born from the hearts of the sea,
Notes of enchantment weave soft and free.
Each creature a note in the grand refrain,
Creating a ballad of joy and pain.

Bubbles rise like a hush of the past,
Through currents swift, our shadows cast.
Guide us onward, O tides of fate,
In the shimmering depths, we celebrate.

With fins as brushstrokes, and shells for drums,
The harmony flourishes, the heartbeat hums.
In the dance of the waves, we find our place,
In the embrace of the depths, we find grace.

So listen closely, let silence speak,
For in quiet moments, the songs we seek.
Together we'll dive into dreams that bloom,
In the shimmering depths, we'll vanquish gloom.

Adrift in the Dreamy Currents

Floating gently in a world of dream,
Where magic flows like a silver stream.
Time unwinds with the ebb and flow,
In this sanctum, we learn to grow.

Each ripple whispers a tale untold,
Of glimmers and shadows, both bright and bold.
As the currents weave through our open hearts,
We become part of the endless arts.

Upon the waves, we find our peace,
As worries of the world begin to cease.
Dreamy currents cradle us low,
In the depths of the waters where the wonders glow.

Adrift we wander, both lost and found,
In the gentle embrace of the heartbeat sound.
Every fleeting moment, a treasure to keep,
In the dreamlike currents, our souls shall leap.

So let us drift in this endless dance,
Where waves are whispers and life's a chance.
In the currents so dreamy, we will reside,
In the heart of the ocean, forever our guide.

Echoes of the Duskbound Reef

As the sun dips low and colors blend,
The reef awakens, where shadows lend.
Echoes of whispers, soft and clear,
Call out to those who are willing to hear.

In twilight's glow, the sea comes alive,
Each creature shares tales through which we thrive.
With vibrant tones and an ebbing light,
The duskbound reef holds ancient insight.

Coral castles framed by the fading sun,
In this sacred space, our hearts become one.
Through currents that pulse, our spirits soar,
In the echoes of tide, we are seeking more.

So brace for the magic that stirs in the deep,
For in every shadow, a secret to keep.
The reef shows the way as the night descends,
With echoes that play, and a promise that bends.

So listen closely to the sounds of the sea,
For in each soft murmur lies harmony.
In the duskbound reef, where dreams intertwine,
We find our own magic in the ocean's design.

Melodies of the Solstice Current

In the glow of the golden light,
Whispers dance on the summer's night.
The breezes carry a soft refrain,
Nature sings in the sweetest gain.

With shadows long and spirits high,
The sun winks low in a sapphire sky.
Crickets chirp to the rhythm of stars,
As dreams take flight like firefly jars.

Along the banks where the waters play,
The ripples hum a mellow sway.
Petals drift on a blissful stream,
Awash in the warmth of a fragrant dream.

Beneath the boughs where the wild things roam,
The heart finds peace, the soul finds home.
With every note of the nightingale's song,
The world recedes, where hearts belong.

So close your eyes to this gentle cheer,
Embrace the magic, let it draw near.
As light and shadow begin to blend,
Feel the melodies of summer, my friend.

Whispers of the Silver Surf

Upon the shore where the moonlight glows,
Waves whisper secrets the water knows.
Crashing softly, they weave a tale,
Of starlit nights and a silvery sail.

With every crest, a sigh takes flight,
Tales of longing in the hush of night.
Mermaids laugh in the foamy spray,
Calling sailors, 'Come out and play!'

The sea is a keeper of dreams untold,
A tapestry woven in azure and gold.
Driftwood holds memories of journeys past,
As time swirls on, both slow and fast.

Above, the heavens unveil their glow,
A dance of constellations, a stellar show.
The stars twinkle in a haunting tune,
While the ocean hums with the rise of the moon.

So lean on the sand, let the breezes tease,
As whispers of surf drift you to ease.
In the night's embrace, find solace here,
Lost in the rhythm, devoid of fear.

Serenades of the Sapphire Horizon

When dawn breaks soft with a violet hue,
A serenade stirs from the ocean blue.
With golden rays painting the land,
Hope unfurls like the sea's gentle hand.

The horizon whispers in shades divine,
As day awakens with a tender line.
Seagulls call to the waking skies,
While sunlight dances in joyous highs.

Each wave, a note in a symphony bright,
Harmonizing with the fading night.
Sails unfurl with a gusty zest,
As adventurers seek the sun's warm nest.

With every breeze, dreams take their flight,
Carried across the sapphire light.
Nature's orchestra plays a serene tune,
Inviting each wanderer to swoon.

So linger awhile where the sky meets the sea,
In this serenade, find your glee.
For every horizon, a promise anew,
Unfolds the magic just waiting for you.

Ballads of the Celestial Foam

In the twilight's grace, the world holds its breath,
As foam-kissed waves sing ballads of depth.
The night unfolds with a silken sigh,
And stars gather close in the velvet sky.

Each droplet sparkles as stories take flight,
Of lovers and legends in the cloak of night.
The ocean's heart beats a rhythm so bold,
Echoing secrets of ages untold.

With each gentle roll of the incoming tide,
The cosmos whispers, a celestial guide.
Footprints trace dreams on the moonlit shore,
As echoes of laughter resound evermore.

The dance of the waves, a timeless embrace,
Each ballad a promise of grace and space.
So join in the chorus, let spirits roam,
For within the foam lies a tale of home.

In the symphony of night, let your heart soar,
And find in the music what you adore.
With every note, weave your story bright,
In the ballads of foam, 'neath the shimmering light.

Verses from the Whispering Ocean

Beneath the shroud of silvery mist,
The ocean hums a gentle tune,
As moonlit waves in shadows twist,
Their secrets shared beneath the rune.

They cradle dreams of distant shores,
In whispers wrapped, the tides conspire,
With every swell, the longing soars,
To find the heart's own wildest fire.

The shells expound their tales untold,
Of sailors brave and storms they braved,
In salty depths, their fates unfold,
In salty tears, their hopes engraved.

Yet in the depths, a calm resides,
Where mermaids sing their haunting song,
In shimmering scale, the magic hides,
A world where time is stretched along.

So let your spirit wander free,
On winds that weave through azure skies,
For in this realm, you'll always be,
A part of vast, eternal sighs.

Lullabies of the Celestial Breakers

The stars above a ballet dance,
As breakers crash on rugged shore,
In night's embrace, they weave a trance,
That soothes the soul and begs for more.

The silver tide, a lullaby,
Whispers secrets to the night,
While moonbeams gently drift and sigh,
In harmony with dreams so bright.

Each swell a promise, soft and sweet,
As galaxies in silence gleam,
The echoes carry, hearts will meet,
In shimmering waves of starlit dream.

Like constellations poised above,
They guide us through the darkened sea,
In every splash, the warmth of love,
Awakens hopes, forever free.

So let the waves your cares release,
And drift upon this azure night,
For every tide brings gentle peace,
In lullabies of purest light.

Songs of the Twilight Tide

In twilight's glow, the waves do sing,
A melody that tugs the heart,
As day retreats and night takes wing,
From golden shores, we'll never part.

The ocean calls with voices sweet,
A harmony of dusk and dawn,
With every surge, the rhythms beat,
As time slips softly into yawn.

In tranquil hues of pink and blue,
The whispers dance upon the breeze,
They tell of dreams and visions true,
Of boundless love that brings us ease.

Each star above a guiding light,
In songs that weave through whispers low,
With every tide, we'll take our flight,
Where twilight's magic starts to flow.

So let the waves crash, fierce and bright,
For in their voice, we find our song,
Together in this endless night,
Where hearts and ocean blend along.

Odes to the Fading Horizon

The horizon blushes at day's end,
Where sky and sea in silence meet,
With every dip, their colors blend,
A painter's heart, a canvas sweet.

In golden rays, the sun dips low,
Kissing the wave with tender grace,
And time slows down, as if to show,
The beauty held in every face.

With each farewell, a promise made,
That dawn will come to break the night,
In softest hues, the light cascades,
Revealing dreams in morning light.

So let the ocean's hymn resound,
In rhythms deep, our souls entwined,
Where every sound of love is found,
And in this dance, the world aligned.

Together we shall roam afar,
On waves of hope, our spirits soar,
For in the fading, we find star,
An ending that forever's more.

Hymns from the Coral Cathedral

In waters deep, where silence sings,
A cathedral of colors, the ocean brings.
With coral spires that reach for light,
Whispered hymns echo, soft and bright.

The fish dance in elegant, fluid grace,
In this underwater, sacred space.
A symphony played by the tides' caress,
A tranquil moment, a world to bless.

Anemones sway with delicate ease,
Drawing strength from the ocean's breeze.
The whispers of shells, secrets of old,
Stories of treasures, waiting to be told.

Beneath the waves, where dreams take flight,
Twinkling starfish in the soft moonlight.
Each pulse of water, a heartbeat strong,
In the cathedral's heart, where all belong.

So dive deep down, let your spirit soar,
In hymns of the ocean forevermore.
Find magic in currents, in shadows cast,
In the Coral Cathedral, peace holds fast.

Nocturne of the Celestial Waters

Moonlight spills on the restless sea,
A nocturne sung, wild and free.
Gentle waves weave their silver thread,
Whispers of the night to be softly fed.

Stars glimmer bright in the velvet sky,
Dancing tides beneath their sigh.
The horizon swirls in a dreamy hue,
Ebbing and flowing, a celestial view.

Crickets chirp on the pebble shore,
As waves retreat, they long for more.
The ocean hums its lullaby sweet,
In the nocturne, where sky and water meet.

Silhouettes of boats drift in the dark,
Star-kissed sails leaving a mark.
Each journey whispers of dusk and dawn,
In the symphony where dreams are drawn.

So let the night hold you in its thrall,
As shadows dance in the deep sea hall.
In the Nocturne's embrace, find your peace,
And let the magic of the waters increase.

Odes to the Enchanted Abyss

Down in the depths, where secrets lie,
In the enchanted abyss, the shadows sigh.
Creatures of wonder, both strange and grand,
Guardians of stories, a silent band.

With bioluminescence, they paint the night,
Flickering in darkness, a ghostly light.
The echoes of ages drift soft and slow,
In this realm where few dare to go.

Ancient shipwrecks rest in slumber deep,
Tales of treachery buried in sleep.
Coral gardens reclaim what once was lost,
Beauty flourishing, no matter the cost.

O God of the Abyss, hear our plea,
Protect the wonders of your deep sea.
For even in shadows, life shall arise,
With every breath, they reach for the skies.

Odes to the depths, where the unknown calls,
In the enchanted abyss, wonder enthralls.
With each whispered secret, a bond we share,
A dance of the ocean, a love affair.

Rhythms of the Misty Lagoon

In the misty lagoon, where whispers dwell,
The water shimmers, weaving a spell.
Moonbeams play on the silvery reeds,
Swaying gently with the timeless needs.

Frogs croak softly in the velvet night,
While fireflies blink, casting soft light.
Reflections ripple beneath the trees,
A symphony born of the evening breeze.

The air is rich with stories untold,
Of ancient spirits, both wise and bold.
In the heart of the lagoon, secrets reside,
Flowing like water, like the turning tide.

Echoes of laughter, of joys long past,
In the rhythms of nature, all shadows cast.
An embrace of tranquility wraps the land,
As the moon hangs low, a guardian's hand.

So linger awhile where dreams take flight,
In the misty lagoon, bathed in soft light.
Let your heart and the waters entwine,
In the rhythms of this world, divine.

Songs of Woven Waves

In moonlit dance, the waves do play,
With whispers soft, they drift and sway.
An ocean's tune in twilight's glow,
Where secrets hide, and dreams can flow.

With every crest, a tale is spun,
Of sailors lost and battles won.
The salty air, a sweet embrace,
As memories linger, time won't chase.

In tranquil depths, the shadows weave,
A tapestry of those who leave.
The stars above, a guiding light,
That sparks the night, ignites the bright.

Through frothy white, the stories gleam,
A symphony of hope and dream.
Each splash a note, with heartbeats near,
The ocean sings, and we must hear.

So listen close, as waves proclaim,
A song of love, a whispered name.
In every rise, in every fall,
Woven waves unite us all.

Echoes of Twilight Seas

As dusk descends, the waters gleam,
In shades of gold, a gentle dream.
The twilight whispers secrets near,
In every wave, a voice we hear.

From shores afar, the echoes call,
With tales of time in shadows crawl.
The gulls take flight, the night draws close,
In twilight's hush, the heart can doze.

With every crash upon the rocks,
The ocean speaks, it never mocks.
Through briny depths, we seek the past,
In memory's tides, the spell is cast.

The playful wind, a lullaby,
That soothes the weary, makes them sigh.
As night unfolds, a dreamer's peace,
In twilight seas, our fears release.

Let every surf, let every tide,
Embrace our hearts, as dreams collide.
In echoes deep, we find our way,
Amidst the night, the dawn holds sway.

Tides of Forgotten Whispers

In hidden coves where shadows lie,
Forgotten whispers softly sigh.
The ocean's breath, both sweet and strange,
In every wave, a world can change.

The sand we tread, a shifting page,
Where memory swims, and hearts engage.
The tide will rise, the tide will fall,
Yet in their dance, we hear their call.

Old stories drift on salty air,
Of lovers lost, of silent prayer.
While foam embraces the land so dear,
The echoes linger, crystal clear.

In twilight's grasp, the past unfolds,
As waves caress with whispers bold.
Through every crash, through every song,
The tides recall where we belong.

So cast your dreams upon the sea,
Let each soft wave set your heart free.
For in the deep, forgotten things,
Awaken softly as the tide swings.

Lullabies from the Ocean's Veil

In ocean's veil, where dreams reside,
A cradle rock of ebbing tide.
The lullabies of waters wide,
Embrace the heart, the soul, the guide.

With tender swells, the night unfolds,
And carries dreams on waves of gold.
Each gentle splash, a whisper sweet,
Invites the weary to retreat.

While silvery moonlight graces shores,
The rhythmic pulse, the ocean pours.
Through rolling waves, a soft refrain,
In every drop, a touch of pain.

So close your eyes, let worries fade,
As starlight weaves a quilt of shade.
In lullabies of seas and skies,
Our spirits dance, forever rise.

For in each wave, a new hope brews,
With tranquil thoughts, we chase our dues.
The ocean hums a calming tune,
Beneath the watchful, silver moon.

Fables from the Ocean's Edge

In the whisper of waves, old tales do sing,
Of sirens and sailors, of treasures they bring.
The moonlight will dance on the crests of the sea,
While shadows of legends drift softly and free.

Seagulls cry out as the tide pulls away,
The stories of mermaids in waters at play.
With shells as their sceptres, they rule by the shore,
Their laughter, an echo, forever will soar.

Each pebble enchanted, a memory kept,
Of journeys once taken, of hearts that have wept.
In whispers of currents, the fables unfold,
The secrets of oceans, both tender and bold.

So gather, dear wanderers, sit by the fire,
And listen to fables that never grow tired.
For in every droplet, a world waits to be,
Where dreams meet the daylight, as vast as the sea.

From depths of the ocean, to skies painted gold,
In rhythm of tides, the eternal tales told.
The ocean's great heart beats with wisdom so old,
And in every wave's crash, a story unfolds.

Enchanted Chords of Dusk Dreams

When twilight descends, soft melodies rise,
The stars weave their magic across velvet skies.
In the hush of the night, dreams start to awake,
With whispers of memory, and hope they will make.

A breeze through the willows carries a tune,
As fireflies flicker, like notes 'neath the moon.
In every soft shadow, a secret is spun,
The lullabies of dusk have now just begun.

With enchantment afoot, the world feels anew,
Each heart beats in time with the symphonic view.
The echoes of laughter, a comforting balm,
In the enchanted dusk, all sorrows feel calm.

Let the chords of the night weave their spell upon you,
As shadows and dreams dance, both gentle and true.
In the quiet embrace of ethereal beams,
The night sings a chorus of glorious dreams.

So rest your weary head and close your bright eyes,
The magic of twilight will carry your sighs.
For in every dim moment, a promise won't fade,
In the chords of the dusk, our dreams shall be made.

Serenades of the Secret Coast

On shores kissed by mist, where the wild lilies sway,
The secrets of ages begin to display.
With tide pools reflecting the sun's golden hue,
Serenades linger in whispers so true.

The cliffs stand like guardians, bold and serene,
While lovers, they gather, where soft waves convene.
In the melody woven by shells on the sand,
A tale of devotion, forever will stand.

As twilight unveils, colors blush from the sea,
The breeze carries echoes of sweet jubilee.
With each gentle rise of the moon in the night,
The coast sings a sonnet of love in the light.

When stars drape the heavens in shimmering lace,
The rhythm of waters creates a soft grace.
Nature composes, with heartbeats entwined,
The serenades echo through ages unlined.

So wander the pathways where ocean meets sky,
In moments like these, let your spirit fly.
For in secret places where legends reside,
The magic of coastlines will never subside.

Voices from the Luminous Waters

Beneath the bright surface, where mysteries dwell,
The voices of water weave stories to tell.
Soft echoes of laughter and whispers of pain,
In depths where the light dances, joy mingles with rain.

Each ripple and wave carries secrets untold,
Of shadows and sunlight, of courage and bold.
A symphony rises, attuned to the night,
With stars in their eyes, the waters ignite.

From the crests of the waves, a chorus takes flight,
In harmony blending the day into night.
In the calm of the evening, a lullaby flows,
The voices of waters in each heart bestows.

So listen, dear dreamer, with heart open wide,
To the songs of the ocean, no reason to hide.
In every soft murmur, a truth seems to gleam,
The luminous waters inspire every dream.

In the cradle of tides, where the moonlight weaves gold,
The voices of oceans, both tender and bold.
Together we'll dance to the rhythm of tides,
In the luminous waters, where wonder abides.

Chronicles of the Ocean's Heart

Beneath the waves, where shadows play,
An ancient tale waits to sway.
With whispers soft, the currents speak,
Of treasures grand, and dreams to seek.

A shipwreck sleeps, in silence deep,
Guarding secrets the sea does keep.
The heart of oceans stirs with grace,
In every tide, a hidden place.

Glimmers of gold in the twilight hue,
Call forth the brave, the bold, the true.
With sails unfurled and spirits high,
They chase the winds that kiss the sky.

From coral thrones, the merfolk glance,
As sailors dare to take their chance.
With laughter light and songs so sweet,
They weave a fate where worlds do meet.

The ocean's heart, a rhythmic beat,
In every wave, a pulse, a heat.
With every splash, a story spins,
Of love and loss, where life begins.

Serenades of the Secret Tides

In moonlit hours, the waters sing,
Soft serenades on the tide's wing.
Secrets linger in the swell,
Of wonders vast, and tales to tell.

The clashing surf on distant shores,
Hides whispers deep like ancient lores.
A dance of kelp, a shimmering light,
Draws wanderers to the heart of night.

With every curl of salty spray,
The ocean calls, inviting play.
With laughter echoing through the deep,
In dreams, the sea holds what we keep.

Starfish twirl on the ocean's floor,
And dolphins leap, forever more.
Their joy becomes a heartfelt sound,
For where they leap, true love is found.

As twilight fades, the world transforms,
In skies of dusk, the ocean warms.
Each wave a note in nature's song,
Serenades where souls belong.

Whispers in the Marine Twilight

In twilight's glow, the ocean sighs,
With murmurs soft beneath the skies.
The tides embrace, in gentle waltz,
A love affair, where time exalts.

Stars appear, like jewels in black,
Their twinkling light guides those who lack.
With every ripple, secrets flow,
Whispers of things we yearn to know.

A lighthouse beams, its watch so true,
As vessels glide on waters blue.
With hearts aglow, they feel the pull,
Of mysteries deep, enchanting, full.

The ocean's breath, a soft caress,
Hides stories grand in its vastness.
Each wave a word, a sacred trust,
A bond that lingers, deep and just.

So listen close, as day departs,
To marine whispers that heal the hearts.
For in the twilight, time stands still,
In ocean's arms, we find our will.

Verses of the Forgotten Merman

Beneath the surface, lost in dreams,
A merman waits by silver streams.
His voice, a longing, sweetly sung,
In ancient tides, where time is young.

His tail reflects the moon's soft gaze,
As memories dance in twilight haze.
With stories woven in seafoam bright,
He sings of love, and endless flight.

In caverns deep, where shadows creep,
The whispers echo, secrets keep.
Forgotten tales of days gone by,
Glimmer like stars in the darkening sky.

A pearl of wisdom in every note,
The merman's heart forever wrote.
For those who listen, truly see,
The beauty in his mystery.

With dreams of realms both near and far,
He casts his hopes like drifting stars.
In ocean's depths, his spirit roams,
In verses sung, he finds his home.